Who is God?

Geri Cruz

Copyright © 2017 Geri Cruz
All rights reserved.

ISBN-10: 1979142238
ISBN-13: 978-1979142236

Table of Contents

Dedication	vii
Front Cover	ix
Introduction	xi
Who do you think God is: the question Geri's mother asked her	1
For those who do not know the story of God and Jesus	5
What the birth of Jesus means to God on a father level	7
Explanation of 'pride is the basis of our relationship'	9
What the true meaning is and was of Jesus	11
Confirmation of a human-divine connection	13
What you may not understand about the death of Jesus	15
Jesus, God, Holy Spirit are One	17
Explanation of the Holy Spirit	19
Why is it possible to know God	21
How does one begin to know God	23

Benefits of uniting with God	25
Why people aren't open to a personal relationship with God	27
True meaning of Easter	29
Does God forgive all sins	31
Does God see everything we do	33
Is any question too silly to ask	35
Why some people ignore God	37
Why do we run from God when we need Him the most	39
What does God want from us	41
Where and how to discover a better YOU	43
How are we ever going to get along globally	45
How God feels about His hurting children	47
Does God take offense to being compared to slipping on a comfortable pair of shoes	49
Why you should never idolize another	51
What would delight and surprise you about God	53
What God wants you to do today	55

Why God doesn't let anyone see His face	57
How one should handle criticism of their spiritual beliefs	59
God's explanation of grace	61
How to love others with compassion who aggravate you	63
Why you should never be offended by what others say	65
Difference between human confidence and spiritual confidence	67
Why people feel unworthy of God	69
Why following God brings you closer to some and separated from others	71
At what age and how you teach your children about God	73
How God's children as a whole are doing spiritually	75
How God wants us to look at the speculation of the return of Jesus	77
What is on God's heart He would like to share	79
Learn something new about God	81
God's final thought to the reader	83

A-Z characteristics of God 85

Other books by Geri Cruz 100

Dedication

In memory of my loving mother

Mildred D. Johnsen

June 24, 1924 ------- May 3, 2017

Who is God?

Front Cover

Outside our bathroom window hangs a cross. Although its whereabouts was a mystery for many years, I would learn later that there are similar cross sightings being reported all over the world since 1983.

In the beginning, my husband and I took the vision for granted. How and why it appeared would be revealed in time.

As the desire to spread the messages became more powerful so did the gathered offenses of others. Often I would awake in the middle of the night and stare out our bathroom window; it was during those lonely nights that I would learn the mystery behind the miracle. Just as God relies on us for strength, He wants us to know we can rely on Him for strength and endurance. The cross is a visual sign He is still by my side. Its presence permeates love, endurance, strength and encouragement, and much more. I know God will never leave me, that we are in this journey together, and *I trust* that everything will work out according to the plan.

Cover design and photos by Arlin Cruz

Who is God?

Introduction

I grew up in Monroe, Washington next to a pig farm. Mr. Breedlove was a Southern Baptist minister. He was a simple man, wore denim-bibbed overalls, and his belly shook when he laughed.

I was never interested in religion, but Mr. Breedlove convinced me to visit his humble church three miles away in Sultan, Washington. I sat in the front row. I became agitated as he yelled out his sermon, after all there weren't many people there. After the service, I asked him why he felt it necessary to yell and in his booming, low voice he explained, "So the people in the back row could hear me."

A small cross hung on our living room wall that read *God Is Love*. Its meaning would remain mounted on the wall for decades before His love in me would blossom petal by petal.

As I sat between Mr. Breedlove and his grandson in an old pickup truck, Mr. Breedlove announced with his unforgettable deep voice, "A rose between two thorns." He would challenge me with thought provoking questions like how do you think the trees and the flowers got here? I told him I didn't know and would scoff off and walk away.

In 1985 my life took a dramatic turn. Just when I thought my life was in perfect order, something was missing. I would stare out our bay window wondering if there wasn't more to life. I had everything on the outside, but something on the inside was missing. That is when I began to seek God. What I discovered was a person that I could not see, that was as real as anyone who stood before me, and the energy of a father figure, mentor and friend unfolded. His wisdom and love filled me.

The petals were slow in forming. I had an inner knowing God wanted me to tell my story based on simplicity and common sense. For over twenty years I refused His request. I gave him every excuse I could think of but He never stopped reminding me, and eventually I surrendered and wrote my first book *Answers from God, Restoring My Soul.*

I proudly presented the book to my mother. Her approval was important to me, but she remained mysteriously silent and her silence deeply hurt and confused me. Months later she acknowledged she was glad I had found my passion. She admitted that when something was overwhelming or too confusing she didn't even try. "How did you get from where you were to here?" In looking back, I can understand her perplexed attitude. Mom was a private person and didn't like to talk about her faith, so I never shared my spiritual experiences with her. "Mom, if I could cut myself open I have a thousand layers of learning I never told you about."

My mother prayed to God everyday for the safety of her children. Talking to Him is the first step in believing He is real. I was no different than my mother in not knowing who God is. It is my intent to help you to get to know the many sides of God by telling you my story and sharing His messages.

When Mr. Breedlove passed, Mrs. Breedlove pulled me and her grandson close and shouted, "God is alive!"

He is alive, and He is waiting for *you*.

Who is God?

Dear God:

My mother phoned me the other day. She asked me, "Who do you think God is?" My response was, "Well, Jesus is His visual and His voice is the Holy Spirit. I have connected with an energy I cannot see. He has changed my life with His messages, and I cannot deny He exists." I think she has a valid question. I would like You to respond to *who is God?*

God: Well, that is a big question. I am your father, father of the universe, and I am an energy you cannot see visually. Open your eyes further and I am all around you, inside you, and able to help you if you ask.

Trusting is a big part of believing. Many cannot believe what they cannot see. Those that expand their heart and mind are open to opportunities others will not.

Our minds are capable of far more than we are using at this time; imagining what you can become and put in the work to get there. Day dreamers are just that, not willing to do the work. You must put in hard work to accomplish your goal and magnify your accomplishments by coming to Me.

Feelings are forever present in your life. Feelings get us in trouble and out of trouble and are powerful forces of what we can accomplish. Expand your mind and emotions to a better you. My feelings can help you expand in confidence and trust by allowing Me to guide you. Are you ready to connect with an energy you cannot see? Are you ready for a father who can fill you with trust and confidence? Are you ready to expand your emotions and your mind?

Experiment, take chances and risks, and see for yourself there is more than what man can see with his eyes. I have been with you far before you were born. *I am one with you and wait for you to ask Me into your life.* I remain dormant until you ask Me into your life.

The mechanics are far too complicated for one to understand. The simplest explanation would defy understanding and only confuse you. Those who know Me can tell others I am alive and real. Those who do not believe may never take a chance. That's o.k. I only want those who are willing.

You are all powerful beings who were born with gifts to be the best you can be. It is up to you to want to discover them and act on them. Being the best is not about things or money. It is about being loved and having healthy relationships that create harmony. Only those feelings feed your soul and sustain you. There is much more to learn about life and self-growth.

I am one with you. I live in you. I want you to trust Me and expand your mind and heart to believe in something you cannot see. I want you to be with Me, to get to know Me, so that I may know you. I want to help you all of your life to live a life of harmony.

Who is God?

Dear God:
For those who do not know You or the story of Jesus, what would You like them to know?

God: I planted an embryo of Me inside Mary. It was part of the plan to help My people. Jesus was custom designed to be an example of Me in human flesh to help his fellow man. I am the very heart of your being. Jesus is My son that was sent to earth as an example of My love and powers. He roamed the earth to share My love for My children.

His voice is My voice (Holy Spirit). It was also designed to be a guidance for man to follow. All what Jesus possesses is available for all humans for the taking *if they believe* and have faith in Me. It was part of the plan when Jesus died that He passed on His powers to all humans.

He continues to live on in those who receive His spirit that is holy.

Jesus came out of Me not unlike sons of fathers on earth.

I want each one of you to know I am available at all times to help you through life. It is a miracle born out of the rebirth of Jesus when He died. *All you need to do is be willing to accept us into your heart and believe the signs and signals I send to you.*

You are able to be born again spiritually, cleansing all errors and gathered offenses of your past and begin anew. It stems from the miracle of Jesus' death.

Love blossoms inside from a bud to full blossom petal by petal. The journey is lifelong and joyous if one sees the positive rather than the negative.

You have only just begun to understand what powers you posses, as My powers are your powers to own.

The joy of the journey is eternity in a space that is filled with honor of oneself. How can I help you understand uniting with Me is the wisest decision you will ever make.

If I threw you a pot of powers, would you take it or would you look at it and walk away?

I have given each of you choices in life to do as you please. I wait for you to look My way and long for you to rely on Me.

Dear God:
What does the birth of Jesus mean to You on a father level?

God: Thank you for asking, few do. They do not realize I have feelings as you all do.

I felt pride as any father would feel. Pride as I witness the miracle of birth as a father. The innocence of a baby is so precious, and I am sorry we cannot hang on to those feelings.

I knew the life path of Jesus. I knew all what He would mean to those paying attention. Standing for all good and all what feeds the soul is a precious commodity. How could I not feel pride?

I watched as He step by step obeyed Me and passed on My teachings. Again, I felt pride. *I watched as He obeyed Me and was crucified for man for the miracle of forgiveness and the washing of sins was put into place.* I felt pride.

Each of you has a life path to help others. You were born with the gift. Are you willing to investigate what you were born to do? Are you willing to come to Me and find out the tools you were born to use?

I am here for you anytime, anywhere. I will communicate in a way you will understand, and I will help you discover your gifts for humanity if only you will ask.

I am not to fear. I love you. I am not a God of fear. I love you. Don't you know I want to be your friend and I have only the best intentions for you that will bring you pride? You must work with Me and make the changes necessary for a better you and a better life. I cannot do it alone.

Pride is the basis of our relationship working together in harmony for our fellow man.

Dear God:
Pride sounds like a direct contradiction to spirit. Please explain what You mean by 'pride is the basis of our relationship.'

God: You are misunderstanding the word pride. Don't think of pride in human terms that speak of boastfulness but rather pleasure in knowing Me.

There is a pride (confidence) that follows the fact someone knows they are worthy of Me, knows I love them and want to protect them, and is willing to receive with pride.

Proud speaks of one's accomplishments. Pride speaks of honor and glory towards God. It is not boastful but an understanding of the pure magnificence of knowing God and Jesus and what they stand for.

Have you ever laid eyes on a beautiful horse, one whose neck is arched with pride, tail extended with purpose, and a prance in knowing who he (she) is? That's pride, knowing who you are in God.

Who is God?

Dear God:
I was wondering the other day, what the true meaning of the sacrifice of Jesus is and was.

God: There is sadness and pride that washes over Me when you ask that question. As a father it was extremely difficult to lose a child. On the other hand, all My children benefited by His death.

Geri: That's what I want to know; the real purpose of His death and how mankind benefited from it.

God: Jesus was and is the human example of who you can be if you follow My teachings. Man needs an image so one can relate. He was and is like Me in an image one can relate to in everyday life.

His presence emulates Me. His walk and talk emulates Me, and His love shows others My love. He shows man how one can live righteously, and how by coming to Me for everything you need I am your answer for your needs.

At the end on the cross Jesus forgave all: "Forgive them for they know not what they do." I forgive those who come to Me for they know not what they do. I show those who admit they have done wrong a better way in which to live.

I want you to emulate Me. I want you to emulate Jesus. Forgive those who know not what they do. Release the chains from your heart and ask for a better way. True forgiveness restores ones soul. A wise heart comes to Me for guidance and wisdom. Forgiveness wipes the slate clean and fresh new beginnings are at your doorstep. It is a miracle one cannot appreciate until experienced.

The beauty is, Jesus didn't die and I knew that. That is what made His so called death acceptable to Me. Another miracle, we do not die. Our true self lives on. Now everyone can have His energy live within them. Those who believe benefit endless blessings of love, comfort, priceless wisdom, friendship and dedication, and a life of understanding, peace, and joy. *The gifts are available to anyone, however, those who do not believe do not benefit.* Taking a chance on something you cannot see is not easy for humans, but those who dare to explore will find magic along the way. Jesus is alive! He is as available to you as He was thousands of years ago.

I'm so glad you asked that question. Anytime I can clarify Myself helps close the gap. Jesus is your visual example of the way one should live a life of righteous behavior. We are who we are by the way we behave.

Dear God:
Thank you for all You have sacrificed in Your life, and most of all losing a son for the betterment of mankind. I cannot imagine such suffering (suddenly I felt extremely nauseas). I'm sorry. I don't know what just happened. Perhaps my body felt your pain.

God: On some level maybe this was true. It was very difficult to sacrifice My son. Sometimes we must accept pain to grow in our soul and evolve to better human beings. It is extremely difficult even for Me, but it needed to be done and I was willing to accept. Acceptance is very important for the value of getting on in life and concentrating on positive future events.

I thank you for your condolences and appreciate you feel for Me. *You do get this is a relationship.* You are wise to acknowledge no visual, and yet you have extracted what you can in faith and a willingness to learn. This is terrific and a concept more I wish to embrace. Teach others they can have what you have if they expand their heart and mind to an energy they cannot see. Powerful things can happen if one is willing to look My way and connect to an energy they cannot see.

We will learn more up the road about this, so let's stop here and absorb.

Dear God:
Is there anything regarding Jesus' death I do not understand or You would like me to know to share with others?

God: Your understanding that His forgiveness on the cross was not just for those who crucified Him but for the whole world. *Mistakes that would be made would already be forgiven.* That's a huge revelation for most.

Also, the cruelty of others must be forgiven. The cross He died on was a symbolic figure that He lived for His father and died for His father. How beautiful. Another example of how Jesus lived, showing all of us how to live our lives.

I think for now that is enough. Your eyes have been opened. Ponder the words, absorb the words so they become part of your weave, so you become the history of Jesus. Teach others they can be like Jesus. Understanding why events take place in history and the meaning behind them all have their purpose and place in current days.

You have all the powers Jesus possesses if only you will ask.

Who is God?

Dear God:
I think of Jesus, God, and the Holy Spirit as One. Am I right in my thinking?

God: Yes, you are right in your thinking. The Father and the Son and the Holy Ghost unite as they stand for peace and love. Many think Jesus as separate from Myself, but He is of the same energy molecular structure as Myself. We are all of the same molecular structure and are one together. Separateness is what divides us and causes differences among us.

If we had the mind set as one, problems would disappear and strength would take place. Knowing that your neighbor is you and you are your neighbor. Dividedness would mentally cease and collectiveness would occur as one. 'United we stand, divided we fall.' The truth is deep in this statement.

Change division into divinity and to this 'Divine self be true.' Get to know yourself through Jesus, God and the Holy Spirit, and know we are in this together. We are here to get to know yourself and be the best you can be through Me.

Who is God?

Dear God:
Do You realize I have never asked You for Your explanation of the Holy Spirit?

God: Seems of little significance at this point. What do you think has guided you the past few years…….The Holy Spirit.

It stands for a spirit that is holy. The spirit lives with each one of us to teach right from wrong. Words, revelations, wisdom, emotions of positive that put you on a path of peace within are all characteristics of the Holy Spirit.

That is only the beginning of a very confusing, complicated explanation that neither confirms you or denies you. You have been and will continue to listen to the Holy Spirit if you believe in Me and ask Me to join you in life.

Who is God?

Dear God:
Why is it possible to know You?

God: The technical reasons are beyond human understanding. That is why faith is important to trust what you do not understand.

Energy never dies. The energy of My son and Me is able to live in you and teach you right from wrong. It was the deal when He died, and trying to explain technicalities would only confuse you. Just know it is possible.

Those that know Me can share with others that there is a life force within that is magical for our taking. *Inviting Me into your life is a start.* That is a first step in believing I am real.

I am only ½ the equation.

Who is God?

Dear God:
How does one begin to get to know You?

God: The only way you get to know God is to spend quiet time with Him. Going *inside* will take you deep within your soul where I merged with you far before you were born.

>You have the powers I possess.

>You have the wisdom I possess.

>You have the love I possess.

Ask Me to guide you through your troubles to show you a better way. Shucking negative in your life is a good beginning. One must reevaluate their life to what works and does not work for them.

Being appreciative for everything you have is also a good beginning. Time flies so fast. Be aware of misused energy, and come to Me for the answer to your needs.

I only want to be your friend.

Who is God?

Dear God:
What are the benefits of uniting with You?

God: What are not the benefits?

1. Cleansing one's soul of pain and anger of unresolved issues
2. Teaching you of My love and powers
3. Teaching you right and wrong by an internal warning system
4. Giving you a perspective of peace
5. Wisdom to know you are on a life path of self growth, and everything that comes into that path is an opportunity to grow wiser, stronger, and more compassionate
6. To learn that what I teach you you will lovingly share with others to strengthen and encourage them on their journey
7. *By believing in Me and Jesus' contribution to the world, will your spirit live on forever in My presence in a world that offers only light*

Who is God?

Dear God:
You have been around a very long time. Why aren't more people open to a personal relationship with You?

God: Because it has been a very long time. Since My existence on earth people have forgotten. If they believed in the bible they would open their eyes to see My relationship with others. It is when I died that people have problems believing.

Have I really lived on? How can I be everywhere at once? How can I believe in something I cannot see?

These are all questions from people who have trouble with a personal relationship with Me. In fact, they make sense in human terms. We are dealing with energy beyond human terms; belief that life goes on after the death of your body, that energy can be everywhere at once, and believing in something they cannot see.

Inside there is a truth to all of it. *If one would take the time to look inside at their own truth they would discover a belief system that has been buried.*

Take time each day to go inside. Willingness is necessary with sincerity. Believing what comes your way, if impossibilities become possible, is helpful. Trusting insight of wisdom is essential. If you believe and use it for good, more will follow. If you use it for material gain, it will cease. There is no room to grow if one wants only to become selfish and full of greed.

I am here for your guidance to become better and live a life of harmony. Each day, with consistency, one will walk into shoes of righteousness and power of oneself.

Reasoning out the concept is for the mind. This is a concept of the heart of knowing a richness of love in one's life. I love sharing My wisdom to help you along the way. Peacefulness is a precious commodity few posses and more should know.

Follow Me all the days of your life, trust in Me, believe in Me from your heart, and take time to get to know Me so I may know you and guide you. I love everyone where you are and who you are, and know you can be who you were born to be with My help and guidance.

Open your heart and allow Me to step into your life to a higher you, one you honor and are proud to live with. I will never leave you.

Dear God:
Teach me the true meaning of Easter, please.

God: Easter symbolizes the resurrection of Jesus. His death symbolizes that we can be born again through the cleansing of our sins. The rebirth of our soul is possible because of what Easter stands for.

Holy, Holy, Holy, merciful and mighty

God in three persons

Blessed Trinity

What does that mean in human terms? *Jesus, God, and the Holy Spirit live inside of you.* His powers are your powers. His teachings are yours to own if one asks.

As I have told you before, Jesus is far more powerful dead than alive. He knew that when He died. He was willing to make the sacrifice for the human race knowing each had the power of evolution in their soul. What the Holy Trinity stands for has not changed. Only now the energy lives *within* verses physically roaming the earth to teach.

Easter symbolizes rebirth, resurrection, and new beginnings. Turn the timer over and see you are full again through Me. Restore old wounds and fresh new growth can occur. Easter is a time of reflection. Who really matters in your life? What really matters in your life? Act on your priorities and restore honor to your life.

Dear God:
Is there any sin You will not forgive?

God: Sins are an admission to doing wrong. If I do not think someone is aware of their wrong doing I am not able to set them on the right path. Sins are an acknowledgement of the wrong path.

I am able to forgive all sins if one recognizes it is a sin. Otherwise, they pay for the destructive damage in their soul.

If life passes you by and you are unaware of right and wrong how do you ever expect to know how to improve your life. One needs to recognize acts of sin and ask for forgiveness; otherwise they remain sins in their soul and are not washed away.

I care for everyone regardless what they have been through. Men of deep corruption are made new again by a conviction of Me. It is time to understand there is more than man can see with his eyes. Powerful things can happen if you look My way and connect with an energy you cannot see.

Set your eyes on peace and allow the progress to begin. Ask for My forgiveness of your sins and acknowledge there are better ways. You are one with Me all of your life, and it is never too late to recognize wrongs. Be willing to change and come to Me for guidance.

Dear God:
Do You see everything each one of us does regardless if You've been asked into our lives?

God: Of course. I live in you. I wait for you to invite Me into your life. I wait for you to discover your true self flaws and all, particularly flaws, that together we are able to drive you in a different direction.

What you become aware of is what you are willing to work with. When you finally see I see, and we are able to work together to resolve issues you are not able to on your own. The stronger the desire in Me to help you the quicker I can get the job done.

I see what you see. I can only fix what you see. Otherwise you are unaware of problems hidden in your soul. Come to Me and I will show you what you need to see, a way out of difficult relationships and times and a better way to live your life. It is not hard to ask Me into your life, but you must have a willing desire and believe in Me. I am your father and want to protect and love you. Open your heart to a better way through Me.

Who is God?

Dear God:
Is there any question You regard as too silly to ask?

God: No. I love it when you ask Me questions. That is how I know what interests you. It gives Me a clue to where you are in your self-growth and how to fix it.

Questions are a wonderful way to show you are interested. Answering them is a joy. Letting Me answer your questions is a sign of trust. If you find My answer correct that creates a further bond. That is trust working one question at a time.

Listening is the other half of the question. Do you just ask and not listen? Know you will find your answer if you are serious. Acting on the answer is the final phase. If you have a question ask it and then act on it. You have the formula you need to change one conflict at a time.

You may not always like the answer you get, but the fact that you come to Me pleases Me. It is what I am here for, to guide you to a comfortable place that brings you peace.

Questions of greed and self-indulgence will never be answered to satisfaction for those asking the question, but those questions are also useful so I may show you a better way that brings harmony to your life.

Ask away. Ask, listen, act.

Dear God:
Why do some people totally ignore You?

God: Fear. Fear of the unknown. Fear of what they cannot see. Fear of looking at themselves. For if they look at Me they must look at themselves. *The fear of standing before Me causes people to ignore Me as if I do not exist.* They hide in their world as if no one is looking and they can continue to do what they know is wrong.

What they do not realize is, that I see everything regardless if they see Me or not. This is the irony.

I will not judge you, you will. I am not to fear, you are. Rest assured I am not your enemy and give you nothing to fear. I am only here to help you and cause your fears to dissolve.

Allow yourself to see Me and know I see you. You are a child of Me, and I only wish to be your father and love you with pure intention. Set your fears aside and ask Me to help you in life, to be by your side to lean on and love.

Ignoring Me does not help you in life but hinders you from becoming who you are together with Me. I hold the magic and wait for you to believe in Me and begin a new life of love and harmony.

Who is God?

Dear God:
Why do we run from You when we need You most?

God: When you need Me most is when you are hurting the most, and your instinct is to run from your troubles. Anchor yourself in Me and know you are on the right track. Running from yourself is running from Me, and that gets you nowhere fast. Calm yourself and calm on Me. It is the hardest to center yourself when you are the most scattered. It is the only way to heal your soul in a timely manner and that is to look inside at 'US.' The fog you are in clouds your vision, and to be as muddled will continue if you do not stop and calm yourself.

Geri: I am trying but my heart is so heavy. My husband and I have lost seven people recently and all have affected us deeply. I have not been visiting You for nearly three months. Taking care of my family seems to be all I can handle.

God: You are doing what you need to do. No need to feel bad about it. Family is your priority right now. What you are missing is the love and comfort I can give you if only you will ask. It's a shift in priorities. A longing for My love. You need it most when you feel you can fit it in least. That is the human way.

Restore your SOUL in 'US' and I will give you SOLACE.

You are My priority, and it is your choice to make Me your priority and know we are in this together.

Dear God:
What do You want from us?

God: To be the best you can be. To be who I designed you to be and act on it. You are born with all the tools you need to be the best you can be. Sharpen the tools I have given you and use them to better yourself. You were designed to serve Me in your own special way. Ask yourself, what comes natural to me? What do I do well? Know that these are the gifts I gave you and they have their purpose. Use them wisely and know they have a higher purpose.

All children are My children, and how you all get along is of utmost importance to Me. *Loving one another is the greatest gift you can give Me.* Displaying a life of harmony shows others a valuable example. The gifts of love are so deep that in a lifetime I could not tell you all of their benefits. LOVE is the answer to life, loving yourself so you may love others. No greater force exists on this earth. Nothing negative can come from love and its actions.

Let Me help you love yourself and dissolve all fear and decay. Restoring your soul anew is the beginning of purpose and peace in your life.

I want you to want Me in your life. I want to help you be all you can be and live a life of joy and love. Your precious life is worth all positive efforts and will be rewarded through the blessings of love.

I want you to want Me to lean on and love so I can help you live a life of peace.

Dear God:
I'd like to continue just sitting with You, asking no questions but listening to what You would like me to know at this time.

God: Allow Me to take the time to tell you how important you are to Me. I never knew as a father I could feel so much love for My children. There is no question sometimes I sit back and wonder why you do the things you do. It is hard for Me, but I know each one of you has to learn your lessons of evolvement in your own time and in your own way.

I would like to ask that instead of criticizing others for their choices in My name, lend a helping hand instead. Listen with an open heart and stop judging, as it is not your place. Concentrate on your own life becoming the best you can be rather than pointing out negative received by your eyes alone.

I note your criticism. I would like you to ask for My help to see your error another way. You are not perfect. Stop thinking you are.

My greatest wish is that you love each other. That means love should pass through you from Me…not venom, poison, judgment, jealousy, or criticism.

The big picture has been lost. Know Me as I may know you to guide you to better ways to live. Allow Me to help you find peace in your heart. Your demeanor will soften as the hardness is erased, and more joy will fill you.

It starts with YOU…not your family, not your friend or your neighbor, but with YOU.

Start today in discovering a better YOU through spending time with Me. Looking for the answers on the outside will never fulfill you, but only the answers on the inside of the truth of your soul which is you and Me together.

Dear God:
How are we ever going to get along globally?

God: With changes few are willing to make at this time. Individuals must look at themselves to see what troubles them. What good is the trouble creating in their life. What satisfaction are they receiving.

The priorities of one's life are nearly upside down at this time. Stop working at what you can gain on the *outside*, and look at what you can gain on the *inside* by coming to Me.

Invisibility is hard for people to accept; accessibility to Me is what they need. I am always available and ready to bring harmony to anyone who asks. Harmony must replace disharmony. *Hardened hearts must let their hatred go.* People must be willing to make changes through their soul and Me. What does not serve you? What parts of your life bring you disharmony? What destructive path have you paved for yourself? Know that if you can pave a destructive path you can pave a constructive path. People will be happier, kinder, more fulfilled with what matters, and their souls will joy at the changes. This is not an effort we can do for someone else, but if we do it for ourselves others will take notice and want the changes for themselves.

They will see the rewards and praises others receive and want some for themselves. No matter what life one has lived, I am here for everyone and I can change anyone who is willing.

Global unity is an ideal goal, and each must begin to work on themselves in order for unity to be accomplished. Unite one another on a daily basis and globally will take care of itself.

Dear God:
It's been so long since I've visited with You. How are You in the midst of upheaval all over the world?

God: Oh Geri, I'll admit it's a lot to take in. People fighting, people uniting, skies and land erupting in destructive and constructive ways. I'm a mix of emotions as everyone is and wish people could know it all has purpose.

Geri: Well, will You tell me?

God: If I told you I'd have to tell everyone, and so many are deaf these days. I must be patient as I ask you to be for the truth to reveal itself, why and how it had to happen.

Geri: I sense Your frustration and loneliness and I want to help. What can I do to help You?

God: Oh Geri---just listening---offering to spend time with Me. It's so helpful to have a friend who cares. Don't ever underestimate a caring friend if all they do is listen: it's called compassion.

Geri: I know God. I've been the recipient of good friends lately and also betrayals which makes the friends even more valued. I want You to know You can talk to me anytime You want. I feel such a sense of sadness from You.

God: I go through sad times like everyone, only I have the privilege of knowing the benefits of the outcome. *I hurt when My children hurt.* I will be alright. Thank you for caring.

Dear God:

The energy I feel when I am with You is like that of slipping on a comfortable pair of shoes. I hope You don't take offense, but a feeling of comfort and reliability and letting go of any pain.

God: How can I possibly take offense to your feelings? I love that you feel so comfortable with Me. Many feel nothing for Me, so no offense taken.

Geri: I really have no questions or concerns today. I feel so peaceful with the wisdom You have revealed to me. I just wanted to visit with You today before I run my errands.

God: Thank you. You don't know how much it means to Me to just *want* to be in My company. I love that.

Geri: The weather has been beautiful the past week. The sun worshippers have nothing to complain about. I get so tired of people complaining about a little rain. If it isn't sun shining every day they're complaining about the weather. Why?

God: Because everyone wants everything to be happy and sunny all the time. *Step back, look at the big picture.* If it only sunshined what would the trees and landscaping look like? Brown and dried up.

This is simple stuff I really have little patience with. I really prefer to unravel more important topics. *It is a simple choice of positive, knowing what good it will do, and negative.*

End of conversation.

Dear God:
I recently began realizing You want me to depend only on You. What is the danger of receiving knowledge from other sources?

God: It's not that I have a problem with you learning in various ways, but if you come to DEPEND on those sources other than Mine that is when I have problems.

Geri: So, what is the problem?

God: *I did not give My son's life for you to idolize another.* Everything your soul needs is taught by Jesus, the Holy Spirit, and Me. I don't want you led down a path of misinformation to trick you into falsehood.

Geri: All due respect God, if it all adds up to truth and is love based how can the information be wrong?

God: As I am an unseen force, there are also many other unseen forces that are not in your best interest. Those are the ones I want you to stay clear of.

Geri: So, how will I know what forces are *not* in my best interest?

God: If you come to Me and Me only, you will know you never need to worry who has your back.

Geri: Sometimes learning about the spiritual world pulse from others helps me know I am not alone in my feelings and that others are struggling with the same problems. There is comfort in knowing others are in the same boat I am.

God: I understand. What I want you to understand loud and clear is, TRUST IN ME. I have told you over and over again that everything will play out naturally, surprisingly, and effectively. Questioning Me over and over again shows Me you have doubt in My abilities.

Dear God:
I seem to be more curious to learn about You. You have shown me many sides through Your messages. What would delight me and surprise me about You?

God: That I love to laugh. I love to smile. I am no different from any of you in that way.

Geri: What can I do to make you laugh?

God: What you do each day. Some days I laugh at your stories you tell others, and mostly you make me smile.

Geri: What is it that makes you smile?

God: The way you've embraced your mission. The way you choose to look at life all for the sake of peace and learning. You give Me the glory and share with others what you have learned. What's not to smile about?

Geri: Thank you. Sometimes I forget all of that because it feels so natural and becomes a daily routine.

God: EXACTLY! BINGO! Yes, that is what the Holy Spirit does for you if you are consistent and sincere. The behavior becomes natural and part of your daily life. Oh, you make Me smile.

Who is God?

Dear God:
What would You have me do today?

God: Do what feels right. Do what needs to be done. Allow common sense to take control and trust. Just as a parent wants to give his child wings, that is what I wish for. Not that you cannot continue to count on Me and come to Me for guidance, but to fly and do so with your own confidence knowing you are flying because that is who you are.

I will always be here for you, but you must take responsibility and learn to become Me. That is what I ask one day at a time. Become Me and all the powers I possess. Use it for the good of man and do not defy Me. Misuse of privilege causes dysfunction and wars. Know that if I can give you the powers I can also remove them.

Geri: Then why did you not remove the fallen angel's powers?

God: The fallen angel had become so powerful within himself it was not possible. The fallen angel, as you say, also has purpose. It is the negative side of life you must stay clear of. Havoc will reign your soul and relationships will suffer. Be aware of a destructive path and know there is a better way. Negative experiences are necessary to remind those who have changed their path never to reenter the same one again. They are necessary for reminders.

What I want you to do today is just be yourself. Life will play out as it should, connections will take place when the time is right, and all will be understood.

Go about your day as you normally would keeping in mind *balance*.

Dear God:

I've read books about people who go to heaven. They have seen Your finger or toe, but they have never seen Your face. Why don't You let anyone see Your face?

God: Because it is not important. The fact that I am alive centuries later and continue to live is what I want people to focus on. What would you have to gain to know My face? How would it help you with your faith? I showed you Jesus. He represents Me.

Geri: It's another curiosity.

God: I appreciate your curious qualities. Your questions have been the bridge in our relationship and trust was the by product. I appreciate your questions. I do not always feel a need to answer them, but I love anyone who wants to know more about Me.

Geri: And I do.

God: Loving Me for who I am, regardless of what I look like, allows you to love Me completely.

If I was ugly would you love Me?

Regardless of what people look like, love them for who they are.

Dear God:
How do I handle criticism of my spiritual beliefs?

God: Thank you for finally asking. This is a very important lesson as you are representing Me. *You handle it with dignity and grace.* Understand how others are woven is not the way you were woven. Their past may be very different from yours, and their reaction to your spiritual beliefs may really be their reaction to their life and what it has taught them.

Know that adverse reaction should not be taken personally. Know emotions to spirit are deep seeded in some and complicated at best. You may be on the receiving end of a whole host of events in one's life that taught a much different view than their own.

Stay strong in Me, knowing that kindness and love is your best defense. Allowing the gate to open to more truth may result in a changed mind and heart. Slamming the gate closed by reacting defensibly only furthers their cause for nonbelief.

You are representing Me. Remember kindness and love and allow those who do not believe to come to Me on their own. Your gracious reaction may be the catalyst.

Who is God?

Dear God:
Explain what grace means to You.

God: Grace is a term in association of Me. It is a form of attitude and behavior on behalf of the individual, knowing they love others with compassion.

Grace is love. When one knows who I am, is filled with who I am, one cannot help but behave with grace.

Judgment, criticism, boundaries of differences are all dissolved. You become one with your friends and neighbors and treat others and yourself with respect, which is the love I feel for you.

It is a softening of the hardening of one's edges. Transformation occurs for only good and harmony. Grace is derived from graciousness: pleasant, kind, courteous, comfort, ease, merciful, compassionate, happy.

One who holds grace lives by My ways.

Who is God?

Dear God:
Help me love those with compassion who aggravate me.

God: Remember, you were once in denial yourself. Remember, you were once resistant yourself. Having someone love you through it would have attracted you to it. Most of all, you free yourself of negative energy. Resistance is within. Resistance is not about others, it is about oneself and conflicts within. So when you have no conflict you no longer have resistance. This is not about you, this is about them and their struggles and about knowing yourself and who you are. Once you have accepted who you really are, those that do not follow will no longer engage you. They simply will not interest you as you only want those who are willing.

It takes time to make the journey, and now you are learning the fine details. Take your time and know this is real, and going what you are going through has value. Never underestimate the stepping stones, as they all have value.

Remember your own resistance once, and give them grace in space to be who they are in their own time and in their own way.

Who is God?

Dear God:
I enjoyed our time together. Well, I really didn't because I had so much on my mind.......Oh!........please do not take offense to what I just said!

God: I never do. *People only react to themselves* (to their own weave).

Who is God?

Dear God:
How can someone who appears to have every confidence feel selfish and unworthy in asking for Your help?

God: Human confidence and spiritual confidence are two separate things. As a person grows they gain confidence by doing right and wrong. They learn what works for them and what does not work in the *outer* world.

Spiritual confidence is entirely different. Many do not go *inside*, guided by their soul which is Me, to experiment and take chances. Therefore, it is a whole other set of circumstances one learns from which is soul based. One has to learn about the benefits of My love and how much I want to help mankind. *One does not feel worthy of Me unless they learn about Me as a person and My powers.* If they did they would know everyone is worthy of My time, anytime, anyway, for anything but greed.

Spiritual worthiness is entirely different than worldly confidence. Jump into the game and know everyone is worthy of Me.

Who is God?

Dear God:
I feel many people feel unworthy of You. Can You tell me why everyone is worthy of You?

God: If only people would take the time to know the many sides of Me they would know everyone is worthy of Me. I love everyone despite what they think of Me, Jesus, or the Holy Spirit.

I made you perfect and hearts become hardened along the way. Self doubt, lack of confidence, fear and other decay rest in your soul causing friction in your life.

Worthiness stems from how one feels about oneself. If you have a hardened heart, I can soften it. If you are angry, I can show you the truth followed by a perspective of peace. If you have muck and tears from past unresolved issues, I can wipe your trouble away if you are willing to do your part.

Recognizing one's own unworthiness and why is the key to change. By not repeating acts of unworthiness proves you have had a heart change, and one by one we can restore your worthiness.

Who is God?

Dear God:
Following You has had its surprises. I find I feel separated from many people and on the other hand feel much closer to others. Tell me the truth.

God: You are learning the inner workings of the soul. The soul will follow its Godly mission. Therefore, uniting with those living the same only makes sense and is comfortable.

Many think they are but are really not. They mean well. It is their interpretation of what they should do. *Many get their guidance from others and not their internal truth.* This is what separates the men from the boys and the women from the girls.

Geri: People will likely take offense to your last statement.

God: The truth is the truth. We are not taught as children how to listen to God, Jesus, or Mother Mary. We listen to others and try to incorporate meanings that function in our lives.

Listening to oneself and following the soul's path is something else. It takes trust and belief above all.

Second, it takes a tremendous amount of courage and patience. The payoff is knowing you are doing the right thing and learning who you are to be the best you can be. Confidence, meaning, purpose and good relationships, are all rewards.

Be glad you have found followers like yourself that understand your cause. Many will see later, as everyone is on the path.

Dear God:
At what age and how would one go about teaching their children about God?

God: When one understands, to some degree, God for themselves that *God Is Love*. Only then should they teach their children what I stand for; love, harmony, peace, and compassion. An individual must understand these tools are within each of us and they are to be used on ourselves and others.

Teaching a child they can connect to an energy they cannot see is hard for adults to understand. As long as it is taught from only good for mankind, it can be taught early in a child's life.

Going to church is only part of God. Helping the less fortunate is only part of God. Going inside and discovering what you were born to do with God by your side many adults have not mastered.

Telling children that impossibilities are possible with God by your side is a wonderful unformed concept. Children are willing much more than adults to believe. Building on innocence for the good of an individual and the good of mankind can only benefit everyone.

The pure joy of discovering that God is alive within each one of us is a good place to start when the children begin to ask. Allow them to experiment and take chances and learn on their own what works for them. They will discover who they really are and begin to trust themselves.

Discover books expanding on the children's questions. Children can teach adults. Children are catalysts to God, as they are less resistant.

Listen to your children. If spirituality is important in the family research to fill the answer, and if it is not make it a priority. The blessings inside are far greater than any outside blessings.

Dear God:
How are Your children as a whole doing spiritually? Are they drawing nearer You or further away?

God: My children are where they need to be for the time being. Spirit cannot be forced. Are you where you need to be? Do you feel that you are doing what you need to do for what you know of Me?

Geri: Yes, in fact I feel very peaceful that I am in the very spot I need to be at this time.

God: That is wonderful. That is what each person needs to ask themselves. People can only act on what they are aware of and then they need to be willing.

My children are where they should be, for what they know, for what they are willing to do. I only want those who are willing. My children cannot be forced to do anything they do not want to do. You know that in your own life. Allow others their space.

Geri: So God, this time and space is all in accordance to the plan You have for us?

God: Yes, all has purpose. *It may differ from one to another but it all comes out in the end; they either accept Me or reject Me.*

They are either for Me or against Me. That is the chaos that will ensue. Two separate forces fighting at great odds each feeling they know what is right.

Geri: Who wins?

God: Depends on who you talk to.

Geri: I am talking to You. In Your eyes who wins?

God: Of course, in My eyes those who accept Me. I cannot protect those who reject Me.

Geri: If they come to You for forgiveness do You still accept them?

God: If their heart has changed, yes, I will accept them. The decision making will escalate and the divisions will be made. It will be clear soon who is for Me and who is against Me.

This is not your worry. Do not live in fear of the future but live with the anticipation of what we can accomplish together.

I can handle this.

Dear God:
Speculation of Your return has people wondering if it is physical or symbolic of inner workings. Please tell me how Jesus plans to return and when.

God: Your questions are premature to your growth. Speculating My return is not how I wish for you to spend your time. Concentrate on how we can grow together, strengthen one another, and help others. Speculating on something whose time has not come is a waste of time and energy. Your needs can be met daily by Me with or without a physical being on My part.

Imagine if Jesus was standing before you. How would you feel? Would you have any regrets? How would you do things differently? Those are all situations to ponder whether I stand before you or not.

My wish is that I want not to have to be an actual physical being for you to discover Me. I live in you, a concept many do not believe or chose to ignore. I am capable of helping you cleanse past pain, guide you to be better and do better, and live in harmony and love.

Don't look for Me on the outside, but follow Me from the *inside voice*. My return should not be what your focus is. Focus on today, how we can cultivate a relationship today, and don't worry about tomorrow.

Dear God:
What do You have on Your heart You would like to share?

God: 'Sharing' is the key word. The way we treat one another is what counts and comes back to us. Know thy will is for good and pass it on. Stay in the mainstream of love and know it grows with time.

Be appreciative in what you learn for the good of man and carry out your goals. Love others as you wish to be loved, and know you are living a life of purpose and meaning.

Propose a new purpose in your life and live it each day. The change may take getting used to but will give new meaning to your day and fulfill your heart. Happiness will replace unhappiness and bring joy to your world. Shout 'Joy to the World' and know it has new meaning for you. Live each day in harmony and know the benefits of health and happiness in your life. Share with others what you have learned and they shall pass it on.

Sharing should be a way of life for all those who follow Me. Gift each other the love you have for Me, yourself, and others. Know I am here for you, and I ask that you share 'the word.'

Who is God?

Dear God:
I'd like to learn something new about You. What would You like to share with Me?

God: It's nothing new, that I love you. I love all of you. That may be hard to understand in your world, but in My world energy never dies.

Imagine if you were a butterfly……..you began not so pretty, not so free. Little by little you grow. Little by little you form wings to fly, and the colors and spots are uniquely yours.

You are not unlike a butterfly whose wings are growing and maturing to fly. It takes time to become strong and support yourself so you will not fall. I am here for you when you do. I am here for you always if only you will ask.

Don't always be looking to be wowed. Just *be* what I have taught you. Become the words I have shared with you. Let the words be part of your weave and gracefully pass on their meaning to those who are ready. *Gracefully grow into a beautiful butterfly leaving behind who you were.* Love is the key to grace and good relationships. You are on earth to evolve each day to the beauty and grace of a beautiful butterfly.

Dearest God:
What final thought would You like Your readers to walk away with about who You are?

God: You now know many sides of Me. You are one with Me and about to learn for yourself who I am and what I stand for.

Don't be foolish and let your knowing end here. I am with you always whether you know it or not, and I can help you anytime and anywhere if you ask. I think you've got it covered if you do not ask.

If you only knew how much I love each of you and want to get to know you so I may guide you.

Please sit down to get to know Me. I want to know you. I love you. I see you struggle and I wonder why you don't ask for My help.

> I am your Father.
>
> I am your friend.
>
> And I want to help you.

Who is God?

Who is God?

The following words or phrases depict characteristics of who God is. They were taken only from the messages in this book and only as they were written. Those that know Him know He is much, much more. Invite Him into your life and discover for yourself who God is and add the words to the list.

A

Accessibility

Alive

Answers for your needs

Appreciation

Available at all times

B

Balance

Beauty

Begin anew

Belief system

Better way

Blessings

Born again spiritually

C

Calm

Caring

Change

Cleanse past pain

Cleansing one's soul

Comfort

Common Sense

Communicate

Compassion

Completion

Concept of the Heart

Confidence

Consistent

Constructive path

Courage

Courteous

Cross

D

Dedication

Delivers

Dignity

Dissolves all fear and anger

E

Ease

Easter

Emotions (Mix of emotions)

Encourage

Energy beyond human terms

Energy you cannot see

Eternity

Everywhere at once

Evolution of the soul

Evolve

Expand in confidence and trust

Expand your emotions and your mind

Expand your heart and mind

F

Faith

Father

Father of the universe

Feeds the soul

Feelings

Free

Friend

Forever

Forgiveness

Fresh new growth

Fulfilled

G

Genuine

Glory

Good

Good for mankind

Good relationships

Grace

Gracious

Grateful

Grow together

Guide you to be better and do better

H

Happiness

Harmony

Health

Healthy relationships

Heal your soul

Heart of our being

Help mankind

Help others

Help you through life

Holy Spirit

Holy Trinity

Honest

Honor

Humble

Hurt (I hurt when My children hurt)

I

Impossibilities become possible

Innocence

Inside voice

Inside you

Internal learning

Internal truth

Invisibility

J

Jesus

Joy

K

Kindness

L

Laugh

Learning

Life force within

Lifetime journey

Light

Lives all around us

Lives in us

Love

Love others

Love yourself

M

Magical

Meaning

Mentor

Merciful

Mighty

Modest

N

New beginnings

New life of harmony and love

New life of joy

O

One with you

P

Path of peace within

Patience

Peace

Personal relationship

Person (know Me as a person)

Perspective of peace

Pleasant

Positive

Powerful force

Power of oneself

Powers

Pride

Protect and love you

Pure intentions

Purpose

Q

R

Real

Rebirth of our soul

Reflection

Resolve issues

Restoration

Restore honor

Restore old wounds

Restore your soul anew

Resurrection

Revelation

Righteousness

Right path

S

Sadness

See everything

Self growth

Self love

Sharing

Shucking negative

Sincerity

Smile

Softening

Solace

Soul

Soul's path

Spirit

Spiritual confidence

Strengthen one another

Strong

T

Teach you right from wrong

Tools

Transformation

Trusting

Truth

U

Understanding

Unseen force

'US' (you and God together)

V

Value

W

Washing of sins

Willingness

Wipe your troubles away

Wisdom

Words

Worthiness

X

Y

Z

Who is God?

Other books by Geri Cruz

Available on Amazon.com,
other retailers and Kindle!

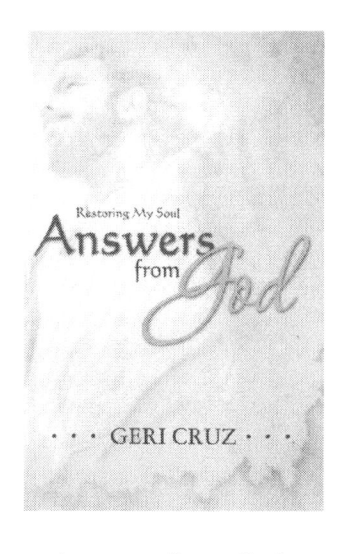

Answers from God,
Restoring My Soul

Guidance from God,
Restoring Your Soul

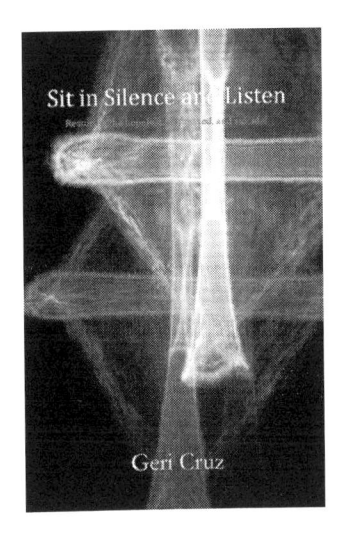

Sit in Silence and Listen,
Restoring the hopeless,
depressed, and suicidal

In 2007, Geri Cruz began receiving messages from God. Despite the fact that she never went to church or read the bible, the words in these teachings will ring quality and truth and meaning for all. Hearts will change and more will be understood. The words are life altering and meaningful for those paying attention.

The messages are a common sense approach to spirituality, simplicity being the key. The by-product is peace within. They are non-denominational, non-cultural, non-gender, because they are non-offensive. They are for anyone who wants to get closer to God.

Who is God?

Who is God?

Who is God?

Made in the USA
Columbia, SC
01 December 2017